The Illustrated Desiderata

words of inspiration by Max Ehrmann

sweet harmony press

© 2022 by Sweet Harmony Press. All right reserved. No part of this publication may be reproduced, stored in a retrieval system, stored in a database and / or published in any form or by any means, electronic, mechanical, photocopying, recording or otherwise, without the prior written permission of the publisher.

Paperback ISBN: 978-1-948713-37-5
Hardcover ISBN: 978-1-948713-38-2
Ebook ISBN: 978-1-948713-39-9

For inquiries for bulk or wholesale orders, contact info@sweetharmonypress.com

www.sweetharmonypress.com

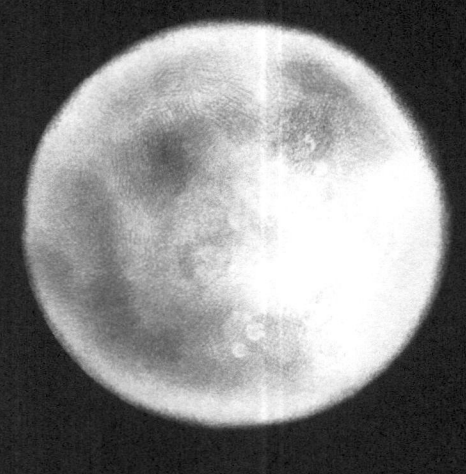

Go placidly amid the noise and the haste and remember what peace there may be in silence.

Speak your truth quietly and clearly;

and listen to others, even to the dull and the ignorant; they too have their story.

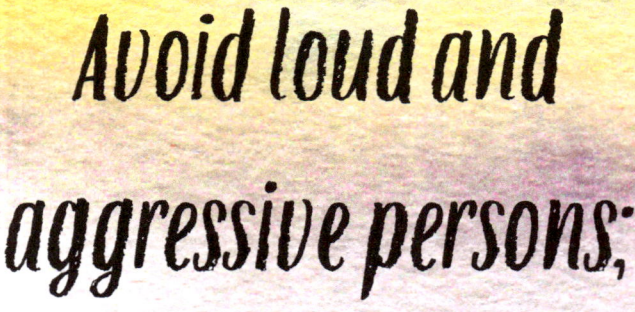

Avoid loud and aggressive persons; they are vexations to the spirit.

If you compare yourself with others, you may become vain or bitter, for always there will be greater and lesser persons than yourself.

Enjoy your achievements as well as your plans.

Keep interested in your own
career, however humble;
it is a real possession in the
changing fortunes of time.

Exercise caution in your business affairs, for the world is full of trickery.

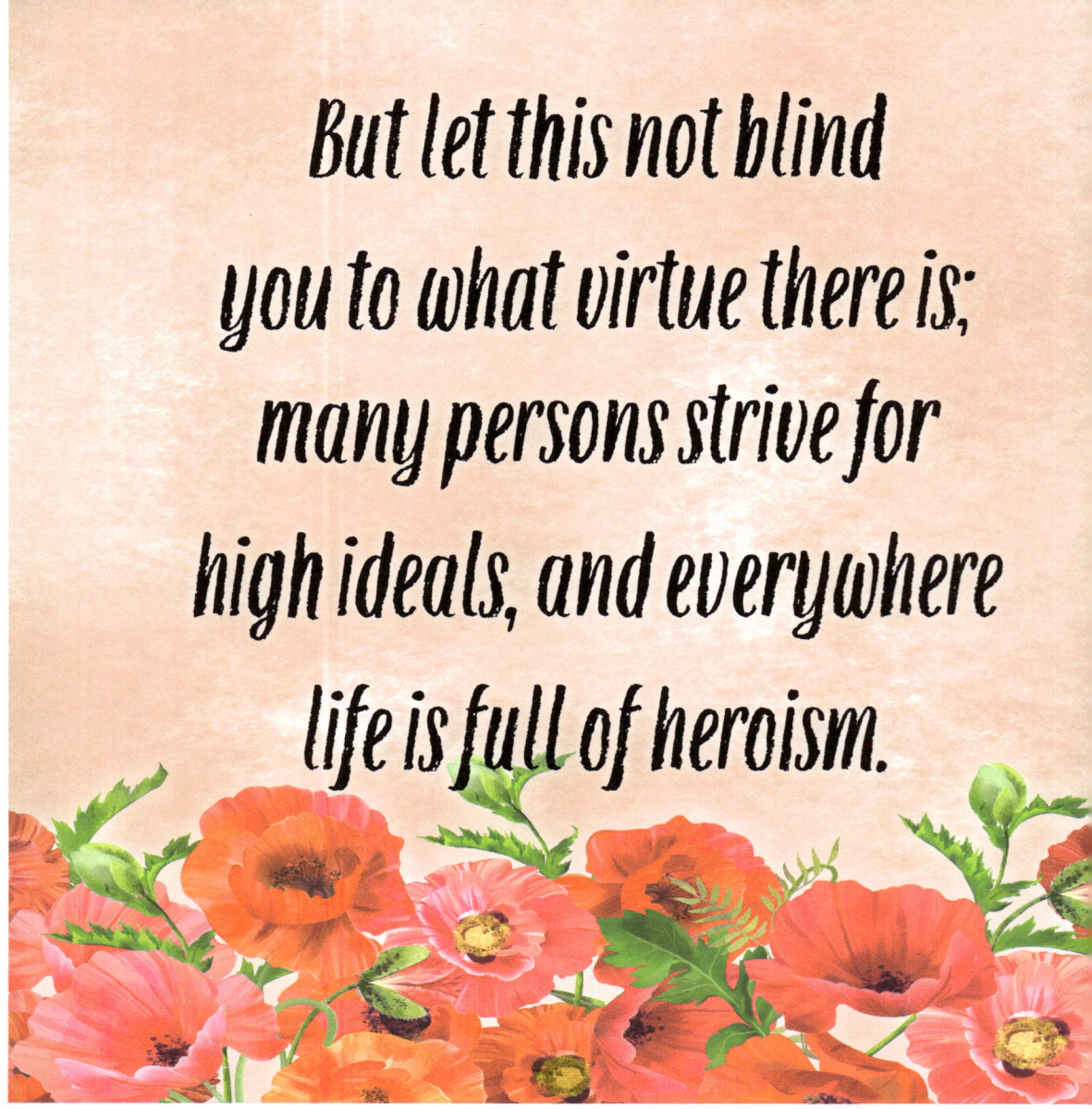
But let this not blind you to what virtue there is; many persons strive for high ideals, and everywhere life is full of heroism.

Especially do not feign affection.

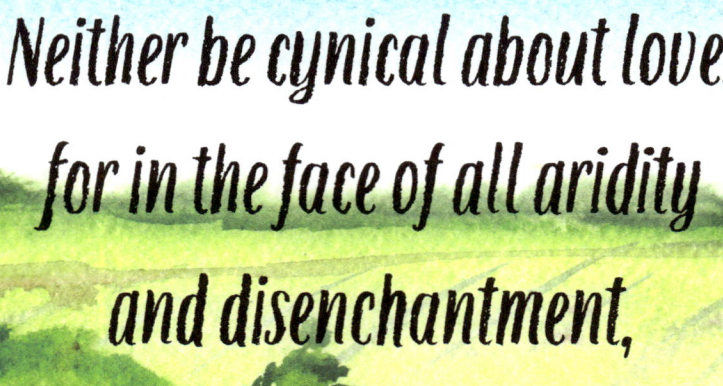

Neither be cynical about love;
for in the face of all aridity
and disenchantment,

it is as perennial
as the grass.

Nurture strength of spirit
to shield you in
sudden misfortune.

But do not distress yourself with dark imaginings.

Many fears are born of fatigue and loneliness.

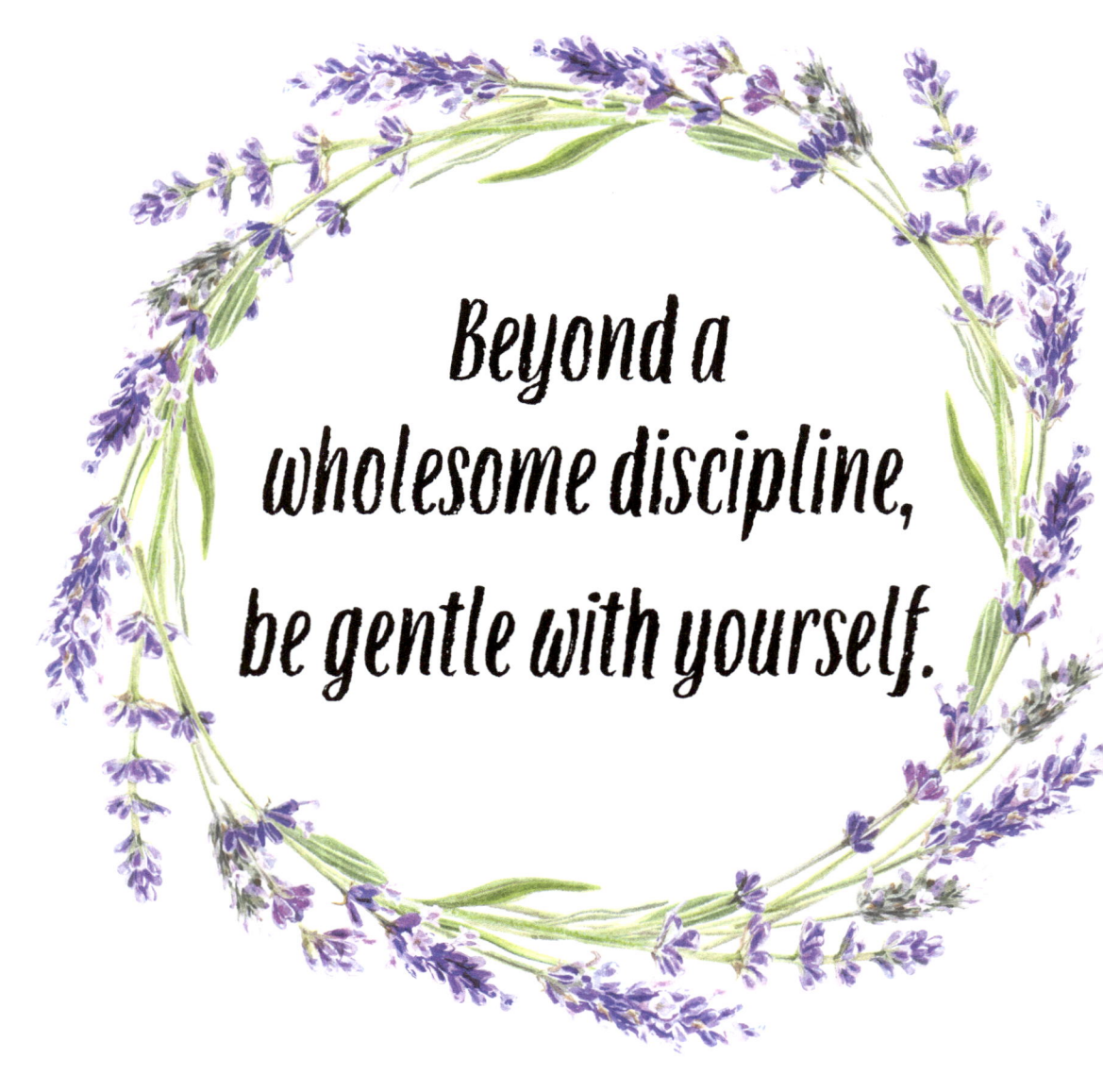

You are a child of the universe,

And whether or not
it is clear to you,
no doubt the universe
is unfolding as it should.

Therefore be at peace with God, whatever you conceive Him to be.

Illustration Credits
All illustrations used with proper commercial licenses through Creative Fabrica.

Cover and Title Page: Busy May Studio
Pages 2-3 Copyright and Intro Page: Beracaink
Pages 4-5 "Go placidly...": Busy May Studio
Pages 6-7 "As far as possible...": Busy May Studio
Pages 8-9 "Speak your truth...": Elena Dorosh Art
Pages 10-11 "Avoid loud...": Elena Dorosh Art
Pages 12-13 "If you compare...": Busy May Studio
Pages 14-15 "Enjoy your achievements...": Elena Dorosh Art
Pages 16-17 "Keep interested...": Busy May Studio
Pages 18-19 "Exercise caution...: EveniiasArt
Pages 20-21 "But let this not...": Elena Dorosh Art
Pages 22-23 "Be yourself": Busy May Studio
Pages 24-25 "Especially do not...": Elena Dorosh Art
Pages 26-27 "Neither be cynical...": Elena Dorosh Art
Pages 28-29 "Take kindly the counsel...": Busy May Studio (sea creatures), KomtsyanTatyanaArt (background)
Pages 30-31 "Nurture strength...": Elena Dorosh Art
Pages 32-33 "But do not distress...": EvgeniiasArt
Pages 34-35 "Many fears...": Busy May Studio
Pages 36-37 "Beyond a wholesome...": Elena Dorosh Art
Pages 38-39 "You are a child...": Beracaink
Pages 40-41 "No less than the...": EvgeniiasArt
Pages 42-43 "You have a right...": Elena Dorosh Art
Pages 44-45 "And whether or not...": Beracaink - background art; TianaGeo - moon
Pages 46-47 "Therefore be at peace...": Blursbyai - Dove; Anna Magenta - sky background
Pages 48-49 "And whatever your labors...": Busy May Studio
Pages 50-51 "With all its sham...": Le Coq Designs
Pages 52-53 "Be cheerful...": Elena Dorosh Art - background, house, trees, Busy May Art - sheep, rabbit, JulaZnom Creative - birds

Ingram Content Group UK Ltd.
Milton Keynes UK
UKHW051946180523
421998UK00003B/33